THE RIDDLE
OF RATIONALISATION

THE RIDDLE
OF
RATIONALISATION

A REVIEW OF THE POTENTIALITIES
OF THE SCIENTIFIC REORGANISATION OF INDUSTRY
UNDER A NATIONAL PLAN

by

L. J. BARLEY

D.S.O., M.A.(OXON), B.SC.(LOND.)

With a Foreword by

SIR JOSIAH STAMP, G.B.E.

LONDON
GEORGE ALLEN & UNWIN LTD
MUSEUM STREET

FIRST PUBLISHED IN 1932

PREFACE

The thesis of this little book is a simple one, however difficult its attainment may be. Briefly it is this.

Since the Great War the methods of production used by or available in industry have made it possible for at least a 50 per cent. greater volume of goods to be produced with the same amount of labour. Theoretically it should be possible for this country to organise in such a way that the standard of living, of wealth, and of profit should be increased in similar proportion. How is this to be done in practice?

I have attempted to analyse the problem —in the main from the point of view of the industrialist on whom the bulk of the burden of reorganisation rests. The financial part of the problem, including the question of public economy and tariffs, has been lightly touched upon, since it has been liberally dealt with in current literature and in the Press.

The scientific reorganisation of industry under British conditions has a small literature, however, and if I succeed in focussing some aspects of the present situation in a manner which will persuade others who are better qualified to take up the pen, I shall be well content.

FOREWORD

The writer of this little book has, both in natural gifts and in experience an unusually adequate equipment for his task. He adds to high scientific and academic competence an eminently practical and business outlook; he has been actively associated throughout with the most conspicuous piece of rationalisation, and of the central planning of industry, which this country has to show. The majority of those who give thought to the present amazing sickness of the world, and the inability of modern industrial society to take proper advantage of its own development and power, are coming to see that extreme and unco-ordinated individualism may not only fail to do justice to our possibilities, but even bring us to the verge of poverty. Nearly everyone is prepared to introduce some degree of conscious co-operation and control in industry—such as prevents municipal and civic affairs from falling into chaos—in order to prevent waste, overlapping and complete misjudgment of economic wants by a large aggregate of uncorrelated decisions. Everywhere there is a feeling that "planning" of some kind must be introduced at different key points in the economic machine to make it function, either at all, or to a better advantage than now. Schemes and suggestions fill the air, and the main questions that emerge are: "Who is to do the planning?" "Do you admit the democratic principle?" "Do you control ultimately by politics and the vote?" "At what stage do you stop, if you *can* stop?" "Is there any place for 'profitability' as a test of survival?" "Is there any scope for individual initiative, and especially for the *new* individual?"

There is a long line between two extreme points—absolute Spencerian individualism and *laissez-faire*, planning nothing, at one end, and Soviet Communism, planning everything, at the other; and we are all busy taking up positions at various points along this line. Some wish to direct the flow of new capital more definitely to particular ends—"directional saving"; others to guide the trade cycle by central and international banking control of the quantity of credit and level of prices; others again, like Lord Melchett, to stabilise and direct the stocks of primary commodities; others to regulate the exact balance of national productivity through quotas and tariff policy; others, again, to control the division of the product of industry by arithmetical and statistical proportions between profits and wages; others to "institutionalise" the products or functions of large public necessities. We are all assuming, without much examination, that the fundamentals of human liberty will remain intact, or that what is left is more precious than our present rag-bag of doubtful rights. We are untangling our way to a new order of economic politics.

Major Barley's contribution contains far more wisdom and suggestion than most works of its length—it wastes no words in clouds. I find it a stimulating contribution to the forward thought of the day. It will certainly annoy, but probably its utility will be in direct proportion to the discomfort it causes; while "for those who like this sort of thing, it is unquestionably the sort of thing they will like." Speaking for myself, I certainly do.

J. C. STAMP

CONTENTS

THE RIDDLE OF RATIONALISATION

CHAPTER I

A DEFINITION OF THE PROBLEM

It is becoming increasingly probable that the period in our history lying between the years 1920 and 1950 will be described as the Second Industrial Revolution. The first decade of this period has been one of the most difficult in our economic experience, and it is well at the end of it to examine critically the progress made, and to concentrate with constructive energy on those avenues of advance in our industrial economy which will be open to us when the world monetary crisis of 1931 has been overcome.

Those who have feared that Britain was being passed in the struggle to regain pre-war pre-eminence and prosperity have invariably focussed our attention upon the unfavourable factors of our progress, such as the unemployment problem, heavy taxation, and sporadic labour troubles. They have neglected both the evidence of progress made and consideration of the unequal nature of our difficulties in comparison with other nations.

What are the facts, and wherein have our difficulties been greater than those of other nations? If they have been greater, it may well be, not only that this country has done well, but that the energy stored up and available is capable of restoring her former preeminence. The British race has never yet failed to follow its star.

Let us examine the position mainly from the point of view of the producer of raw materials, manufactured articles, or transport facilities, i.e. the employer of labour. It is only by increasing *his* efficiency progressively that the employment and general prosperity of the nation can be maintained. In our Press, and in public life, too little emphasis is laid on the vital fact that industrial efficiency, in the widest sense, is as necessary for progress as good government.

The problem, in the first place, is to find an ultimate standard by which efficiency may be measured, and put briefly, it will read somewhat as follows:

"*The maximum profitable production of goods in every industry.*"

This is a definition of 100-per-cent. efficiency in the national economy. It is doubtful whether six industries in the country could estimate the extent to which they are efficient if judged by this apparently simple standard: it is doubtful whether three of our industries have the final goal before them.

The purpose of our speculative study of future development must clearly be:

(1) *To find a scientific method of estimating the maximum profitable production of goods attainable.*

and

(2) *To find a basis for reorganising our industrial system in order to attain maximum efficiency.*

The task is one involving the development of a new Industrial Science which will convert commerce and industry into units regulated according to laws more or less exact, and, moreover, laws which will be understood and applied by those responsible for the administration of production and distribution.

Their application will tend to replace the slow-working action of economic laws by controlled decisions, based on knowledge of the causes and extent of fluctuations occurring in

B

the normal course of expanding prosperity, and of the correct measures to eliminate them.

Unfortunately the difficulties which have to be overcome by Industrial Science at the present time are not merely those of establishing a new standard of living within the British Empire. Before this can be done a world crisis in finance must be overcome by international action, which will require the broadest insight of which our leaders are capable. It is therefore necessary to consider whether both problems may not be carried a long way toward solution by the use of scientific methods.

CHAPTER II

THE FIRST POST-WAR DECADE

The nineteenth century had witnessed the industrialisation of Great Britain, and the picture of material progress it leaves in our minds is sharply defined. The outposts of the Empire had been widely extended, welcoming the arrival of British emigrants and sending back an ever-increasing stream of raw materials, precious metals, and food, thus foreshadowing the completely dominating position which Empire trade will occupy in the future in the national accounts. The standard of living increased four times during the century. It appeared that if political and administrative skill could so satisfy the aspirations of sections of the Empire as to enable them to determine their own affairs, and of industrial labour so as to better its share in the proceeds of industry, the prospect of the twentieth century was a fair one.

In the years immediately preceding the War there was one other cloud on the far horizon —the rise of Germany as a competitive industrial nation. Looking back, it seems clear now that this competitive factor would ultimately have wrested more for the Germans from the other industrial nations than a mediocre victory in war could have done. The national consciousness of the German nation expressed itself not only in military and naval preparedness, but in production on an increasing scale, and in the spread of the arteries of commerce in competition with Great Britain throughout the world. That particular cloud was displaced by a typhoon. The War brought about a violent change in every factor of our industrial evolution, and we are still struggling, almost blindly, to recrystallise the situation.

There is something very ponderous about our great national movements. We leave reluctantly the methods and aspirations of the past. It is difficult even to forget that well on in 1915, when British batteries in Flanders were firing a rationed daily salvo, the industrial slogan at home was "Business as Usual," instead of "Reorganise for War." It is perhaps only natural that the answer to a pressing problem should be sought in the accumulated experience of the past and that we should be diffident about too much thinking ahead, or "Vision." When the War ended, the slogan became "Reconstruction," and the criterion of success was the return to pre-war conditions. To a great extent even at the present time the future possibilities of industrial enterprise have been obscured by the unemployment problem, and it is only being dimly realised that by means of improved machinery and organisation, together with the potentialities of the new industries which have been built up since the War, production and national wealth can be made to increase with speed.

It is now commonly agreed that the problem to be faced by most of our industries is that of Scientific Reorganisation, and, in order to understand what has brought us to the necessity for reorganisation, we must consider some of the new conditions which have sprung into being or become intensified in other countries since the War. Apart from monetary factors, they constitute the competitive conditions which British industries are facing at the present time.

I propose to demonstrate that, by dint of scientific reorganisation, it will be possible for us to reassume priority of place in the world markets even though we are faced with a lower scale of wages in some countries and vast tariff-protected productive capacity in others.

Competition with Low-Wage Countries

In the first place, it is widely believed that British industry cannot compete in many directions with the low-wage conditions in several Continental countries. This is true to some extent if one deals with the past, but what of the future? Germany, Belgium, France, Italy, have all gone through a period of violent inflation, and before it is possible to assess comparative competitive conditions on a permanent basis we must examine the progress and results of the inflation itself.

In the case of Germany the process of inflation was carried to the farthest limit that could be borne by the industrial system without chaos supervening.

It was forced on Germany by the Treaty of Versailles. Payment of Reparations to the Allies, in kind and in money, could only be made by the export of goods, ships, rolling-stock, live stock, securities, and foreign balances, which were owned by individuals and companies, who had to be compensated for their surrender by the German Government. Compensation could only take the form of German currency. There was no alternative to the printing press, and currency fell

in value day by day, month by month, for
nearly five years, until a sum of money which,
in pre-inflation days, would have liquidated
the German National Debt, would not keep
an artisan in the necessities of life for a week.
The word "milliard" was as easy to print on
a currency note as the word "mark." The
value of the paper mark fell to twenty
thousand million to the pound sterling. It
seems fantastic that such a Rake's Progress
could not be arrested before all the consequences had been realised. The economic
results of inflation can easily be set out in
broad outline. They amounted to a revolution.
The German National Debt and all War
Loans were wiped out. Industrial debentures
became worthless and were paid off with the
price of a postage stamp. Fixed interest-
bearing securities lost all value, while the
ordinary shares of industrial concerns which
carried the equity of business rocketed to
tremendous quotations in paper marks, since
they received the whole profits of industry.
They represented the ownership of goods,
factories, and foreign balances: solid assets.
The inevitable results were not realised by
the outside world for years. America, and to
a lesser extent Britain, spent vast sums in

the speculative purchase of German marks, hoping for their restoration to higher value, and these sums helped to meet the Reparation payments.

The German rentier class, the professional classes, and indeed the bulk of the middle classes, lost everything before they realised what exactly was happening to them. It would be possible to digress at great length on the social consequences of German inflation. The industrial consequences were no less profound.

The inflation period was one of unparalleled activity. The banks were willing to lend paper money for the extension of production. Labour was unprecedentedly cheap. Manufacturers— in spite of a growing realisation of the inevitable crash, and the ever-present difficulty of obtaining raw materials—undoubtedly built and operated more machinery and new plants each year than Britain did during the whole period of the struggle to replace the pound sterling on a gold basis. Wages in terms of English currency fell at times to three half-pence per hour for a skilled man, and the services of a research chemist could be hired for, say, £40 per annum. It was natural that the competitive power of German Industry, owing to these low-wage conditions, should become a byword, although in point of fact there were compensating difficulties in the way of lack of commercial organisation overseas and post-war antipathy which prevented a wholesale use of low production costs so as to re-establish German export trade on a broader basis than had existed before the War.

The Origin of Rationalisation

It would again be a digression to examine these difficulties since they no longer exist, but it is necessary that consideration should be given to one aspect of them in order that the reorganisation of industry by scientific methods may be traced to one of its sources. The inflation period in Germany probably gave rise to the conception of the Rationalisation of Industry, and in this manner. If the Finance Ministry and the various industries of Germany had not created some sort of organisation to control and advise their members in carrying on foreign trade during the progress of inflation, great confusion would have occurred. It was necessary that goods which were produced at a fraction of the price they would realise abroad should be sold to the best advantage in order that Reparations might be paid, and necessary raw materials required from abroad paid for and distributed fairly among the industries requiring them. A purchaser of German goods in the Allied countries deducted 26 per cent. from his payment to the German manufacturer and paid it to Reparations account. The manufacturer was reimbursed by the German Government in paper marks. In addition, the manufacturer had to give up a proportion of his receipts in foreign currency to the Government—a proportion depending on the amount of raw material he required from abroad. The more imported raw material he employed, the less good currency he surrendered. It was necessary to obtain permits either to import raw material or to export manufactured goods, and a tremendous amount of supervision and organisation was necessary to control the whole business. For each industry a Committee of Control (Aussenhandelstelle) was appointed—about sixty were created in all—with members largely drawn from within the industry.

There is little doubt that as a result of this organisation there arose in the minds of the German industrialists a vision of the efficiency which a united industry could give. Larger groupings took place, and the chief industries of the country—coal, steel, chemicals, gas, potash—became organised into much larger if not entirely national units.

In 1923 the mark was stabilised, and the gold mark, or guaranteed rentenmark, reappeared. The inflation boom was over. Wages remained at a low but not at an absurdly low figure in comparison with British wages, but they began to approximate to ours, and any advantage they gave was counterbalanced by a shortage of working capital and by the fact that Germany had still to reorganise export selling effort in order to regain foreign markets. It is significant that German competition of a permanent character became strongest in those manufactures where reorganisation and amalgamations had taken place.

In Belgium, France, Czechoslovakia, and Italy the same processes went on. Inflation was followed by currency depreciation and very low real wages. Stabilisation left wages on a lower level than British wages. Part of the National Debt was wiped out. Taxation, both national and local, remained extremely low, as compared with our own. Industries such as steel and textiles undoubtedly flourished at the expense of the corresponding British industries, but, on the whole, no greater advantage was taken by these countries than was afforded to them by the chances of inflation.

With the lapse of Great Britain from the Gold Standard in September 1931, most of the remaining advantages of the "inflation" countries disappeared, and, without inflation, Britain can for a while obtain the increased trade afforded by being able to sell more cheaply in competitive markets than the countries which remain on the Gold Standard. The main sections of this book deal, however, with permanent conditions, and our advantages, although they may hold for several years if we can readjust the balance of trade, cannot be regarded as entirely permanent, although they may be retained in part.

Competition with High-Wage Countries

In the second place, it is sometimes the experience of our manufacturers that they have difficulty in competing with American goods in export markets—in some cases even in the home market. Such competition is almost invariably the case where commodities are manufactured in America in enormous quantities, by standardised mass-production methods, and under scientific control. The reader is asked to concentrate on these three factors because they constitute high competitive power and ensure low production costs, even though the wage-level may be higher. It is not to be thought that these ideal conditions obtain throughout American industry. Indeed, there are wider variations in efficiency than in England, and many industries could not remain prosperous and pay high wages, as they do, without heavy tariff protection. It is, however, a significant fact that tariff protection has hardly been required by some sections of the American motor-car industry, because the requisite output and efficiency have been attained to reduce domestic selling prices below the production costs of their competitors. There are evidently lessons to be learned here, and we shall see whether they cannot be applied to our own industries.

A Datum Line

The first post-war decade ended with a truer conception of the nature of the problem which lies ahead. As a result, each section of the financial, industrial, and commercial community should be able to concentrate on constructive work without the waste of time and resources in which a hesitating and diffused policy must result.

Great power of leadership is required in order that the younger men in industry may be fired with enthusiasm to create, administer, and find markets for the reconstructed units of production for which the raw materials lie ready to hand, and to develop from them advantages for every section of the community.

The financial and commercial experience and reputation accumulated by this country over the last century, combined with a labour force of great intelligence and skill, and the economic advantages of a well-developed island situation within an Empire of unbounded resources, constitute material factors which are possessed by no other nation.

CHAPTER III

THE DEFINITION AND SCOPE OF RATIONALISATION

The word itself was hardly known in 1925. It has become hackneyed since; but even so its meaning was at first little understood—so little that in 1929 financial depredations carried out in its name culminated in the gaoling of one of the most successful of its false prophets. The Hatry disaster typified the ignorance with which the problem of rationalisation was approached by directors and shareholders of some of the smaller industrial companies. A financial amalgamation was labelled "Rationalisation" regardless of the industrial objective of the company. What a contrast to such operations is provided by amalgamations such as, for example, Imperial Chemical Industries, Limited! The annual reports of that company indicate the creation of a truly national or rather imperial industry along the lines of a predetermined policy, which includes the manufacture in this country of raw materials and new products formerly imported from those countries which had temporarily surpassed us, and also of commodities for export on an equal footing with the other great chemical companies of the world. Reading between the lines, one obtains a picture of a far-flung selling machine for these home-produced products, neglecting few of the available avenues for the expansion of trade and yet deferring to the necessity of production in the Dominions by means of associated companies. Other industries offer equally favourable examples of scientific organisation —of vision which has clearly in mind the maximum attainable profitable production of goods together with the betterment of the standard of living of the workers and fair dealing with the purchasing public. There has been little talk during recent years of exploitation of the public by so-called "Trusts," and the explanation is that the principle of sharing the profits of industry between workers, staff, shareholders, and consumer has become a firmly established practice. Public opinion is too strong and social forces are too evenly balanced to allow wide deviation from the principle.

A true conception of Rationalisation is in process of emerging from the problems of the last decade. It will be put into practice in proportion to the extent to which Industrial Science becomes a true science and not merely a question of personal experience, of business instinct, and of following a trend. There can be no turning back. The growth of knowledge arising from the application of statistical science will enable men of ability to control productive units of increasing size and to co-ordinate their activities with related units of production and distribution. Their success will inspire others and will create a demand for teaching facilities in order that the young men entering industry may receive adequate training, and from these two factors a true Industrial Science will emerge. Britain has always provided scientific leadership, and it can be confidently expected that the emphasis which is now being laid on the question of industrial reorganisation will produce in time great thinkers who will co-ordinate discovery and teaching in this field.

Enough has been said to enable us to define Rationalisation as "*The scientific reorganisation of industry with the object of obtaining the maximum profitable production of goods and a higher standard of living for the community without unfair exploitation of any one class.*"

It is not a Utopia which is pictured. The

scope which is possessed by industrial science to-day is definite. Raw materials, modern methods of production, technical staff, and in many cases machinery, are available for sufficient production to increase the average standard of living in the country by 50 per cent., and it should not be an impossible task to evolve plans which will enable the goods which can so easily be manufactured to be distributed—i.e. sold to our own population and at the same time to enable a favourable trade balance to be maintained and even increased in order to pay for the additional raw materials which will require to be imported. These two questions of distribution of goods and of the national balance of trade are the essence of the problem. Responsibility regarding the adjustment of the trade balance must be taken by individual industries, and it is no longer possible, owing to the trade restrictions imposed by nationalistic aspirations, for this country to continue to purchase raw materials and food in an unrestricted fashion from countries which have neither the purchasing power nor the will to take more than a little of their requirements of manufactured goods from Great Britain. In many cases a strongly integrated industry can, over a period of years, organise the production of its raw materials within the Empire, and it can ensure that imports of manufactured goods coming within its range of products are reduced to a minimum. The extent to which tariffs may be necessary to maintain a satisfactory trade balance is still a matter for experiment and merits close discussion in relation to the scientific reorganisation of industry, but it does seem clear that in some cases a prohibitive tariff would give the home manufacturer the total United Kingdom market, with the consequent high level of production and lowest attainable cost. Given these, there is no reason why prices should rise—indeed, they must fall in order to give new impetus to consumption—and there is little reason why export trade should not be increased.

National Units of Industry

The great scope of reorganised production and distribution can be realised in the main by the creation of national industries—imperial in their outlook and having complete knowledge of every phase of their business throughout the world. Initially some industries may contain too many companies for unity to be brought about, and intermediate steps such as joint research, statistical and selling organisations may be necessary. But until such national industries exist, little progress can be made towards a permanent scientific control over economic forces which have from time to time, and especially since the last great slump, been too much for mankind.

Organisation into national sections of industry is not invariably necessary, or even desirable. In most industries there is room for the small specialist firm, for luxury production, and for the artistic productions of individual craftsmanship which have done so much to build up the reputation of British goods in the world markets. Even in these cases, however, much may be done by co-operative marketing between the larger and the smaller organisations.

Historically speaking, it may be but a small step to the time when industry and finance are organised in all civilised countries on a national basis in such a manner that economic forces can be kept within bounds by negotiation, and both price-level and production be kept under scientific control to a far greater extent than they are to-day. The whole mechanism of industry becomes immensely simplified when bigger units come into play. A country which has such large units of production will have a commercial policy relating to every country in the world—a rational policy capable of realisation within a reasonable time and capable of negotiation within a few months to the maximum advantage of the participants. A country cannot expect to attain an objective which requires scientific organisation throughout every phase of production and distribution if most of its industries are built up of independent units each dealing with a special branch of business, none having a definite objective or policy except to make a fair return during the current year, and none possessing the resources to compete with the huge corporations which may be organised in other countries. The case seems clear, and yet it is more the rule than the exception that our manufacturers spend the half of their energy and resources in competing with their good friends and competitors on the other side of the home town.

The difficulties lying between the present position and the ideal set out above are extremely great and must not be minimised.

It is argued by some that vital changes will not come about in the less progressive of our industries for twenty to thirty years—that is, until a new and more enlightened generation is in control. Such a view may be regarded as pessimistic. The tendency towards scientific control of industry is well advanced, and a few of our larger and newer industries are already using methods which approach to the true scientific attack on the problem of maximum profitable production arranged in conjunction with the corresponding industries of other nations.

One of the greatest stumbling-blocks to progress is the existence of the small and inefficient business with limited output, the direction of which is carried out by rule-of-thumb methods, with no attempt to contribute to the problems of reorganisation which are facing us. In the opinion of enlightened observers it is impossible to take such a business into a plan of rationalisation, since its demands for a share in the capitalisation of a larger organisation would be too great to be faced, in view of the fact that its machinery is obsolete and worthless and the industry could not carry the remuneration which has been drawn in the past by the owners. If this is the case it does not constitute an argument against scientific reorganisation. The process will be delayed until inefficient concerns have been eliminated by the competition of the more efficient. There will arrive a stage, however, when the affairs of such businesses are in such low water that they can be persuaded to transfer their production to efficient units and to accept a reasonable measure of compensation for their withdrawal.

The tendency towards economic nationalism in all civilised countries is now so definite that it will clearly continue. Hitherto its effect has been in restraint of free movement of goods and has contributed largely to the existing state of over-production in the world. However, it is true that the ultimate needs of mankind are sufficiently great to absorb any production of the commodities of everyday life which can be visualised, and, on broad lines, it seems probable that, given the state of national industries throughout the world as outlined in this chapter, a much freer interchange of goods could be promoted by international co-operation and negotiation.

The main objective, therefore, is to intensify existing methods of rapid production to an extent which will add 50 per cent. at least to the normal exchange of commodities. Countries which are in the main producers of raw material will export more of their commodities, and they will, in spite of incipient growth of home manufacture of consumption goods, be in a position to take far more of those goods requiring the industrial skill of the older manufacturing countries.

Higher Living Standard or Leisure

Since the methods of production are tending more and more to utilise less labour, there are only two alternatives: either the world must realise rapidly a considerably higher standard of living with existing hours of labour, or it must cut down hours of labour progressively. Either policy involves scientific planning on an international scale, and, of the two, to aim at a higher standard of living is more consistent with the progressive urge towards better things which is inherent in mankind. It is, moreover, the easier problem to solve.

CHAPTER IV

THE WORLD ECONOMIC CRISIS

The crisis in the world's economic affairs reached in the autumn of 1931 transcends in importance and danger any international problem which has presented itself for solution in the past. It is no longer sufficient for each country to adopt panic methods of balancing budgets and meeting or avoiding liabilities which, in general, are in restraint of trade. It is only by the production of consumption goods in increasing volume throughout the world that prosperity can be restored permanently, and it is impossible to see a radical increase in consuming power unless prices of raw materials and of securities of all kinds are raised.

The depth of the economic depression is due to loss of consuming power caused by the tremendous fall in values between 1929 and 1931. Private individuals, industrial corporations, and employees generally, have all lost money to such an extent that they are unwilling to engage in anything but necessary commitments. Taxation in every country tends to become heavier to compensate for the loss in revenue entailed by this fall in the price of commodities, and so decreases again the spending power of the population. The operation of the economic forces which have corrected past depressions is either hindered or prevented by the vast question of war debts and post-war international credits, or it is postponed for an unprecedented time owing to the existence of extremely abnormal stocks of raw materials, the consumption of which cannot be stimulated by low prices owing to the loss of income and capital by every civilised community. In addition, the great nations of the East have lost much of their external purchasing power owing to the low price of silver.

If losses have been so heavy throughout the world that an increase of exchange of consumption goods appears to be indefinitely postponed, what action can be taken? It is useless for individual nations to attempt to solve their own problems and to expect prosperity to return without the general prosperity of the world being readjusted also. International action is, therefore, necessary on the scale which has been discussed in the preceding chapter. But how is such action to be taken when national industries do not exist which could present their case and evolve their plan of action? To build up such national industries is likely to take at least from ten to twenty years.

The answer to this question is, that we cannot hope to deal with the crisis in the comprehensive manner which would be possible if the industries of all the chief industrial and raw-material-producing countries were scientifically organised, but that a very important commencement can be made with such industries as have adopted scientific methods or which are so relatively simple in their world organisation that the action of their units may be controlled and answered for by their respective Governments.

A Higher Price-Level

The Report of the Macmillan Committee on Banking and Industry merits close study with a view to building up a basis for such international action. Its most important recommendation deals with the necessity for stability of prices of raw commodities at higher figures than those then ruling.

"275.—Thus our objective should be, so far

as it lies within the power of this country, to influence the international price-level first of all to raise prices a long way above the present level and then to maintain them at the level thus reached with as much stability as can be managed."

Since the date of the Macmillan Report further catastrophic falls have taken place in the price-level (see table opposite). The primary producer, holding on tenaciously to his livelihood, is tightening his belt, working without profit, and making every available economy. Whether worker or shareholder, he is going without luxury goods, and reducing his requirements of necessities. The resulting unemployment in industrial centres again reduces the demand for manufactured articles and primary commodities and prices fall further.

When and how can the vicious circle be broken? In the normal way, within two years of the commencement of a slump, low prices would stimulate production, low money rates would make working capital available to industry and activity would once more take an upward turn. Surplus funds would flow to undeveloped countries from creditor countries to find a higher rate of interest. It would be transferred in the main as manufactured

COMMODITY PRICES

	October 31, 1929	June 23, 1931	Friday, September 18, 1931*
WHEAT—per cwt.			
English	9s. 9d.	6s. 3d.	5s. 6d.
Canadian No. 3 ..	12s. 3d.	5s. 9d.	5s.
Argentine	10s. 6d.	5s.	4s. 3d.
MAIZE—per cwt.	8s. 9d.	5s. 6d.	3s. 6d.
BEEF—per 8 lb.			
English long sides ..	5s.	6s.	4s. 4d.
Argentine hindquarters (chilled)	4s. 9d.	4s. 1d.	4s. 3d.
LAMB—per 8 lb.			
New Zealand	5s. 10d.	5s. 3d.	5s. 7d.
RUBBER—per lb.			
Plantation crêpe ..	10d.	3d.	2½d.
COPPER—per ton			
Standard	£71 10s.	£35 10s.	£30 10s.
COTTON—per lb.			
Middling American ..	10d.	5·20d.	3·75d.
WOOL—per lb.			
Queensland scoured merino	36d.	26d.	24d.
Australasian medium ..	18d.	11d.	9d.
FLAX—per ton			
Fine quality, water retted	£120	£95	£90
Low grade	£62 10s.	£35	£35

* The last quotations before further falls were obscured by the depreciation in sterling.

commodities, and, again, activity would be increased by means of international loans and credits.

Thus the Macmillan Report states: "309.— We think that the first measure towards the restoration of the international price-level must necessarily be taken on the initiative of the creditor countries, and that it must consist partly in a greater willingness to buy and partly in a greater willingness to lend."

The constitutional remedies are failing for the time being. Tariff walls, war debts, and short-term loans, combined with lack of confidence and lack of political and economic security, are preventing the natural advantage of cheap money and a superfluity of potential credit in the United States and France from exercising their curative effect. When the United States arranges the direct exchange of bags of wheat for bags of coffee from Brazil, it is time to consider whether there may not be some virtue in again employing the commercial methods of the Phœnicians. The regulation of the balance of trade and capital requirements of States amounts in the end to scientific barter, and regulation of production to the amount required for the maximum amount of exchange of goods for goods, and goods for credit, which can be justified by the state of the art of bartering.

I have put forward in the previous chapter a theory that the exchange of goods can be regulated and increased much more easily if fewer but more efficient industrial units, preferably organised on a national basis, are dealing with the situation. Now let us see how quickly the scientific action which they would take can be applied to raise the price-level of primary commodities and restore world confidence.

I. First of all, what is the situation?

(i) Enormous stocks, amounting in many cases to between one and two years' normal world consumption, are held in some cases by Sales Cartels, in others more loosely, and are financed to a large extent by the banks.

(ii) Primary producers are struggling hard to reduce costs, but diminishing output and continually falling prices have made it difficult for any profit to be made.

(iii) In spite of this, stocks are not falling because demand has decreased at such a paralysing rate owing to world monetary factors.

(iv) Although the price position would ultimately correct itself, and, indeed, shows tardy signs of so doing, this might not happen until the world is one-third unemployed, by which time financial and even political dislocation would have supervened in many countries.

(v) A rise of 40 per cent. in the price of primary products is necessary to bring a return to confidence and prosperity.

If the picture is as black as it has been painted, international action must be taken quickly to force up the price-level.

II. Secondly, what are the essential steps in the attainment of world control of prices?

(i) Stocks of the chief commodities must be strongly held. In this and in regulating production primary producers, Governments, and banks must all share the responsibility.

(ii) Stocks must be reduced over a period judged suitable for the conditions to a figure which constitutes a safe reserve for all contingencies.

(iii) An agreement must be arrived at between Governments to enforce a restriction of output in order that normal stocks may be attained.

(iv) Prices must be stabilised for long periods and only moved as a result of scientific study.

(v) Speculation must be prevented.

(vi) By international banking co-operation, possibly through the Bank of International Settlements, the problem of credits, exchange, and gold reserves must be adjusted to take care of these operations.

The action set out above involves a meeting, with plenary power, of representatives of all Governments, of primary producers, and of bankers of the chief nations. It would succeed or fail in forming a world plan for every main primary commodity within three months and the world would have a chance of rapid recovery to a degree of prosperity hitherto undreamed of.

Such a policy may seem to be a negation of the tenets of free commercial enterprise with which we are imbued. And yet, is it? Control of prices is aimed at by every cartel which exists, and the only additional factor in the suggestion is the power of each Government to enforce production quotas on its nationals. It is certain that the effect would be to double the share value of the capitalist and to effect the security and comfort of the worker in the industries concerned.

Assume for a moment that such a plan has succeeded. What then?

We have accomplished for the first time in the history of mankind the regulation of production of primary commodities, we have arranged for a stock to be held which is large enough to ensure us against excessive demand or temporary failure in supply. We have eliminated speculation, and we have placed the primary producer in a position to re-enter the markets of the world, to purchase necessary manufactured goods, luxuries, and equipment. Best of all, confidence has been restored. Creditor countries will now lend again and industrial activity can be resumed much nearer to the capacity of our plants.

Can we not extend the scientific method to obtain greater stability of prices of manufactured goods?

It can be done if we have national industries or cartels efficient enough to go into negotiation with the backing of their Governments. By efficiency is meant knowledge of the world situation, of the rightful share of trade to be obtained, and of the price which will give maximum attainable profitable production of goods. Certain industries almost come up to our ideal already without the fear of accusation of anything but fair dealing being aimed at them. Explosives, soap, alkalis, provide examples. Fertilisers (especially nitrogenous fertilisers) and artificial silk might be added to the list without much difficulty, and regain their right to a fair return on capital, in conjunction with measures to increase consumption in every country. One point it is necessary to mention. It is essential in an efficient world plan that a halt should be called in setting up new enterprises until the older established units are running on fuller load with minimum costs. It should be a principle of economic nationalism that plants are not set up until the consumption capacity of a country will ensure minimum costs. Otherwise maximum attainable profitable production will not be carried out and the highest standard of living cannot be reached. When a country has a large enough consuming capacity to justify a factory, the manufacturers of older nations by arrangement should share in the enterprise and receive payment for their experience. So are efficiency and experience both utilised and rewarded.

Silver

One further measure of outstanding importance tending to regain world prosperity would be the remonetisation of silver. China has a currency based on silver. India, which until recent years had the same, possesses a large concentration of the metal in the form of the accumulated hoardings of her vast population. In the greater part of the rest of the world silver has become a mere commodity, and its price has fallen to a fraction of its former value. What is the effect on trade? The external purchasing power of the myriad peoples of the great Eastern countries has been cut in half and their savings have been diminishing in value at a rapid pace for some years.

It is proposed by the bimetallists that those Governments which are affected (e.g. India, Great Britain, Mexico) should enter into an agreement to buy and sell silver only at a definite price in relation to gold, the figure being fixed at about double its price in September 1931.

There are, of course, arguments to be raised against the proposal, as, for instance, the effect on internal prices in China, but there is no doubt that the effect of the remonetisation of silver on the export trade of the United Kingdom and other countries with India and China would be both immediate and substantial. New purchasing power would have been created not due to unregulated inflation, but to a new and controllable source of credit. The gold-shortage problem outside the United States and France would be correspondingly less.

It does, therefore, seem to be common sense that international action to decide the question of revaluation of silver should be taken without delay.

CHAPTER V

STUMBLING-BLOCKS

Before considering the principles of the application of industrial science in order to obtain the maximum profitable production of goods, it would be wise to consider to what extent the faults in our present organisation must be corrected. The result of successful achievement should be a far greater volume of exchange of goods in spite of the growth of economic nationalism, and it is necessary to have monetary and tariff systems throughout the world working efficiently and not so much as at present in restraint of trade.

The following factors require consideration and action before a stable basis can be afforded for scientific reorganisation.

(a) Reparations

Reparations payments by Germany have been responsible for a great deal of confusion during the post-war reconstruction period. As shown in Chapter II, they led directly to the inflation period in Germany and indirectly to inflation in other countries. It must have been clear to the economists and politicians at the Versailles Conference that reparations could only be paid in goods, and that it was impossible for Germany to create an annual exportable balance in goods and, at the same time, rehabilitate her internal organisation. In fact, reparations have been paid by the creditor nations—chiefly the United States—granting loans to Germany. When the flow of credit to that country ceased in 1931, it became impossible for further payments on reparations account to be made. The amount of credit lent to Germany during the past six years on long or short term exceeds considerably the amount of reparations paid, and it will be the utmost that Germany can accomplish to pay interest and amortisation on these loans if we assume that further loans are not granted.

It is a fantastic anomaly that world conditions would have been rectified within a few years of the War if America had paid reparations in gold, instead of Germany being expected to pay in goods, which to a large extent were unacceptable to the allied countries, since they did not create a corresponding outflow of goods from those countries.

It is impossible to resist the conclusion that further

Reparation payments are impossible unless creditor countries are willing to allow the whole amount to remain in Germany as long-term loans.

(b) War Debts

The same observations might be applied to the question of war debts, which represent capital loaned mainly by America, but also largely by England, to other nations. This capital did not fulfil its normal purpose of development in that it was used for munitions of war and destroyed, leaving a burden of debt which in the normal course could only be paid by the creation of a favourable trade balance on the part of the debtor nations and by the reception of America and Great Britain of goods in repayment. The United States has been unwilling to accept goods in greater proportion than she exported, and Great Britain has recently become unable to continue this policy of accepting goods freely owing to an increasingly unfavourable trade balance and reduced invisible earnings from shipping and financial services.

Again, it seems clear that war debts must be cancelled, or scaled down to a figure justified by the willingness of the United States to receive goods or

*to invest money in the debtor countries at a regular
rate.*

(c) Tariffs

The free exchange of goods has received
heavy blows since the War through the tendency of almost every country to build up as
many industries as possible within a tariff
barrier. This policy of economic nationalism
has been due to three main causes: (i) The
effect of the War in making each country rely
more on its own resources; (ii) the necessity
of creating a favourable trade balance; (iii) the
spread of knowledge of productive methods,
combined with a desire to increase the standard
of living.

The United States has one of the highest
tariff barriers, and has been able to manufacture within these barriers a volume of goods
which not only warranted a high standard of
living but enabled American manufacturers,
by mass production, to export certain types of
goods in competition with the rest of the world.
The United States cannot, however, have it
both ways; she cannot possess a favourable
trade balance and at the same time avoid the
actions to which a creditor nation becomes

liable. Her favourable trade balance must be either invested abroad or taken into the country as manufactured goods. We have already seen the impossibility of payments being made to America on account of war debts unless the same willingness is manifested.

This policy of economic nationalism has gone so far that it cannot be resisted, and any international action on the tariff question must take account of it. The United States has led the van; European countries, and ultimately British Dominions, followed. Russia presents an example *par excellence* of a country which aims to have a completely self-supporting economic system. It is now probable that Great Britain will adopt a policy of protective tariffs, which will obtain much more of the home market for her manufactured goods.

We must, therefore, accept it as inevitable that nations will retain their tariff systems, and that the effect of tariffs in preventing the free exchange of goods must be overcome under our scientific industrialism by some other method than that of free trade. Every country produces certain raw materials and manufactured goods which others may not be so well qualified to make, and which, in any case, they cannot make cheaply enough owing to lack of natural resources, cheap labour, or industrial skill. There are many goods in this class, moreover, which it is not necessary for a country to produce to satisfy its aspirations in the direction of economic nationalism. Under existing tariff systems it is impossible for two countries to exchange goods of this nature because tariff systems are too inflexible and prevent importations either way. The tendency, if each country had high tariffs, would be to do without the superior article available by importation or to manufacture it less efficiently. It is probable that, from the point of view of employment and efficiency in both countries, it would be desirable for such articles to be exchanged. To bring this about is impossible unless by a process of barter, or, alternatively, by close negotiation on tariff adjustment between the two countries.

An International Conference on tariffs should, therefore, take place which would discuss a freer exchange of goods based on investigations on these lines.

(d) Tariff or Free Trade for Great Britain

From the point of view of the scientific reorganisation of production, it is of extreme importance that the question of a tariff system for Great Britain should be decided without undue delay. The temporary relapse from the Gold Standard has indeed given many of the advantages of a tariff, in that it stimulates domestic production and encourages exports. The temporary effect of this relapse is that we must pay more by, say, 30 per cent. for everything which we import from countries which remain on the Gold Standard or whose currencies do not further depreciate in relation to gold. We therefore tend to produce the goods which have thus become dearer in this country. At the same time, we are in a position to obtain a higher price in sterling for everything we export, and to increase our competitive power and obtain orders for our goods to the extent by which we are willing to sacrifice the proportion of the advantage which the depreciation in our currency gives us. The result has been a certain stimulus to manufacturing activity, but the effect of such action is not equivalent to the imposition of a tariff, since all products entering the country, including raw materials and food, increase in price to the manufacturer and consumer, and also because there is always an element of uncertainty in the basis for commercial negotiations in view of the fact that currency values may alter within short periods of time.

It must be remembered also that, ultimately, stabilisation has to be faced, either at the original value of the pound sterling in relation to gold, or at some lower figure. In either case, and especially in the former, the process is a difficult one, and entails sacrifice of some of the business which may be obtained at the commencement of the period of instability.

The question of a tariff, and its nature if imposed, seems likely to be decided within a reasonable time, and the effects can be taken into account by producers in any scheme of reorganisation. A permanent and stable tariff policy is necessary to give our industries an incentive to create strong linkages with such export markets as they can obtain under the tariff system imposed, and especially with the Dominions. It will also induce them to extend the spirit of efficiency back to the production of their imported raw material requirements in those countries most closely linked with British trade.

CHAPTER VI

A NATIONAL PLAN

How to find employment for two and a half million workers.—How, moreover, to increase the standard of living of the whole community by 50 per cent.! Have we a hope?

Would it not be better to abandon such absurdity of thought and leave our industrial system to change gradually by the slow process of evolution? That line of thought has brought mankind into the present tangle, and it must not be allowed to happen again.

In converting the energy available from coal into power, at least 75 per cent. goes up the chimney and is lost. It is wasted in spite of one hundred and fifty years of scientific achievement. Twenty years ago 85 per cent. was lost to the atmosphere, so that the process of gaining efficiency is accelerating. Industrial efficiency is a parallel case. Seventy-five per cent. of our ablest endeavour is lost in unproductive competition, in overlapping and confused striving.

The possibilities of the situation are obvious. We want to produce every commodity in such a way that each element entering into its cost delivered to the ultimate consumer has been subjected to most stringent efficiency tests. The manager of the small business cannot even apply such tests, still less command the desired results. If the ideal is to be attained, every phase of our chief industries must be working in unison, so as to obtain maximum efficiency, lowest attainable cost, economic distribution, large and progressive production with proportional price reduction, adequate financial reserves, and a fair return on the capital actually utilised.

This cannot be attained by the old system of internal competition. Erstwhile competitors must find the common basis of efficiency together, and it is this factor which forms the greatest stumbling-block to progress, because although there lies in most of us confidence in our national power to rise to a crisis and to find a temporary solution to any difficulty, the majority do not believe that any body of Englishmen can follow a common policy towards a far-distant goal.

Central Co-ordinating Action

Some form of central action is required as a focus for reorganisation—a body of experts working in close relation to the Government to co-ordinate, advise and plan for industry, but not to control and without executive powers.

To organise our trade scientifically with such speed as is necessary to meet the present emergency, it is necessary to make co-ordinated effort, industry by industry, in—

(a) Building up a picture of the maximum attainable trade by pooling accumulated knowledge;

(b) Preparing a plan of reorganisation which could attain that trade; and

(c) Setting out the requirements for the plan in the way of organisation, new capital, tariffs, etc.

I suggest, therefore, that the Government should institute a Commission on each industry or portion of industry consenting to the procedure, staffed from the industry itself and from the banking interests, but having a neutral chairman, appointed by the Government. It would be guided by an expert advisory department, which would provide the secretariat, prepare the report of the Commission, and build up a store of knowledge for the guidance of industry and the Government. Its functions could perhaps be defined by the title National Advisory Economic Planning Department. *It would also deal with Empire trade problems.*

Some such regulated procedure is vitally necessary, for the full meaning and possibilities of Scientific Reorganisation are not generally understood, and cannot be realised without co-ordination and the most expert advice available.

It is as necessary to produce a finished plan for the reorganisation of selling effort and for the organisation of production as it is to carry out the financial amalgamation.

The essential difference between these proposals and the partial measures of rationalisation which are sometimes taken is that the PLAN should precede ACTION. The difference is fundamental.

What are the functions of the Government in such a vast measure of reorganisation?

It gives to industry the services of an expert Planning Department, and provides such facilities for new finance, education, co-ordination of tariff policy with that of the Dominions, Consular and Statistical services, as may be required when the situation has been clarified. The reorganised industry, however, remains free from Government interference, and the Government free from responsibility for its

E

conduct. There must be no compulsion, but a general infusion throughout our industrial life of Leadership, Efficiency, and Knowledge.

As we have already pointed out, one of the greatest difficulties to be overcome is the resistance of the manufacturer to the idea of becoming a small factor in a larger unit. This is inevitable, and can only be minimised by the organisation of the industry in such a way as to give positions of importance and responsibility to the efficient, and by the elimination of the inefficient with suitable compensation.

Finance

The next greatest difficulty, and the one requiring the chief consideration of the Government, is that of Finance.

An approved PLAN would show wide extension of trade and great saving in manufacturing and selling expenses. The estimated profit under the PLAN should, at the worst, provide suitable reserves and interest on the old and the new capital. If it does not, the old capital must be ruthlessly written down. Additional profit would be devoted to the increase of wages, the increase of dividends, and the reduction of prices.

The new capital required might be raised in a uniform way by debentures secured as a first charge on the assets and profits of the industry, the Government guaranteeing the interest over a period of years. A small proportion of these debentures might be issued to the Treasury in order to provide for payments under the guarantee and make the scheme self-supporting.

It is recognised that for some years a considerable portion of the national savings would be absorbed, but, on the other hand, by judicious co-operation with American finance, a great deal of the money necessary could be raised in that country and inflation in England avoided. Better still, finance might proceed from an International Investment Corporation and Development Trust, which might be constituted by international subscription, to finance not only such schemes as would arise out of this proposal, but also similar schemes in other countries. Such an idea is undoubtedly gaining ground as a means for the redistribution of gold now massed in America and France. If put into effect, it would also take care of the financial measures necessary in order to raise and stabilise the commodity price-level as suggested in Chapter IV. It would certainly provide a rallying point for international co-operation between national industries.

Once accepted by industry as a basis for exploration, the above proposals should rapidly succeed. Once accepted by the Press, in order that public opinion could be educated, there would be wide co-operation throughout the Empire for a doctrine of efficiency and scientific reconstruction. The scheme is self-supporting, and involves little, if any, additional cost to the State. Its effect on unemployment would be rapid. It should, if handled rightly, unite all the immense reserves of ability, initiative, and effort in our people, which tend to lie dormant unless they are fired by a crisis in their affairs such as exists to-day. Our post-war generation would have found a guiding principle by which to regulate their life-work.

Planning

We have thus outlined a method by which industry could be reorganised, mainly by its own effort. It is necessary to point out what information each company would have to provide before the PLAN of reorganisation could be prepared, because there is naturally unwillingness to disclose details of costs and markets which may be transferred to competitors. This unwillingness to impart information to a neutral body, combined with disinclination to subordinate personal interests to the common good, is so important that it is mentioned again with an appeal to British industrialists not to allow initial suspicion to stand in the way of national necessity.

The organisation of an Advisory Planning Department has been envisaged. It would require expert sections to deal with the commercial, technical, and financial aspects of any investigation. It might be desirable to have, in addition, a further Consultative Committee composed of acknowledged leaders in banking, commerce, and industry. The Planning Department would act in relation to individual firms in the same confidential capacity as a solicitor or chartered accountant acts towards his clients. It would have to do without accurate figures where companies refused to supply them, but would, in such cases, build up the PLAN on such general statistics, information and assumptions as might be obtainable. In nine cases out of ten a workable PLAN could be presented to the Commission.

The following general requirements are set out:

(a) Relevant financial details.

(b) List of products.

(c) Existing costs of production.

(d) Existing sales to various markets.

(e) Competition from other countries by markets.

(f) Possible costs of production, assuming—
   (i) Standardisation.
   (ii) Concentration of similar manufactures in most efficient plants.
   (iii) Extension of markets to an estimated attainable figure.

(g) Estimated saving in selling organisation.

(h) Estimated saving in purchasing raw materials.

(i) Estimated attainable sales with the reduced costs available.

(j) Details of research being carried out.

(k) Personnel available for the new organisation.

(l) Possibility of manufacturing raw materials in this country or in the Empire.

(m) Possibility of extending trade in Dominions or foreign countries by local manufacture or association with local manufacturers.

The Advisory Department would then prepare a PLAN which would have the following main features :

(i) Reorganisation of production (including purchasing and research).

(ii) Estimate of attainable costs, sales, and profits.

(iii) Reorganisation and extension of selling organisation and propaganda.

(iv) Financial reorganisation (including plans for raising new capital.

(v) Personnel.

(vi) Tariff questions.

(vii) Effect on employment and on wages.

The PLAN having been agreed by the Commission, it would be passed back to the industry to be carried out. The Government would exercise no compulsion in the matter, and, unless a Government guarantee were required by the industry for interest on debenture capital, no control would be exercised over the financial structure of the new company except by Company Laws universally applied in order to prevent abuses.

The Government, on the mass of general information in the possession of the Advisory Planning Department, would support the economic structure of industry in questions of tariffs, taxation, Empire development, education, and statistics.

CHAPTER VII

OVER-PRODUCTION, UNDER-CONSUMPTION, OR SCIENTIFIC ADJUSTMENT

"There is no need to talk of over-production until the last Hottentot has become a millionaire." This piquant over-statement by a prominent industrialist indicates that he, at least, saw no difficulty in distributing manufactured goods in much greater quantities than they are to-day. The picture conjured up is one of a world in which vast productive capacity has been built up by machinery to an extent that the capital represented would be sufficient to make every inhabitant of the world a millionaire, some of whom would deign to occupy themselves for a short period daily in pressing buttons to make the machinery work. It is ardently to be hoped that the rate of scientific progress will not be high enough to force this mechanical world upon us; but, on the other hand, we are faced with the urgent situation that it is possible to produce considerably more goods of almost every kind, and that unless production and economic distribution are re-organised, unemployment must continue at a high figure. It is unnecessary at the present time to consider making a large number of millionaires, but no one can deny the advantage of placing the average standard of living so much higher that every workman who is willing to give an honest day's labour may have a well-furnished and comfortable house to live in, with a chance of buying a small car, a radio set, and attractive clothes for his wife and children, and also of obtaining education for the latter of such a type as to give them equality of opportunity with the children of those even more fortunately placed. It is not our purpose to enter into a political discussion, and this is not at all a question of socialism. It is a problem of making a capitalist system operate in the United Kingdom in such a way as to cure unemployment. In the course of solving this problem a great deal of wealth will be created, and it is to be presumed that the distribution of such wealth would follow similar lines to those obtaining at the present time.

It is not only a question of distributing goods amongst our own citizens. Raw materials have to be imported, and they cannot all come from the Empire.

Increasing quantities of raw material must be paid for by an increasing outflow of goods in payment for them, and it is on this point that all schemes of increasing production break down unless they are combined with a corresponding increase of efficiency and lowering of costs.

Now let us come to the root of the matter and state that finance, industry, and distribution to-day are under-organised and working at perhaps only 40 per cent. efficiency. This is responsible at the present time for the apparent crisis in our affairs.

We tend to starve in a world of plenty.

It would be possible to give examples of high efficiency in manufacturing organisations in this country. Yet none are so striking as the principles consistently put into operation by Henry Ford in the process of developing his great organisation. He discovered a new principle, as great as any scientific discovery—a principle involving high wages, but demanding the utmost in efficiency from labour and from machines. The way to counteract a slump and to extend both domestic and export sales was to make more and more automobiles in order to obtain lower costs and to sell at a proportionately lower price. This degree of efficiency was not confined to the motor-car trade. It was extended to many of the necessary raw materials. Plate-glass was required; it could not be afforded at its existing price, and a new and largely mechanical process had to be evolved which gave substantial cost reduction. The net result was that twenty years of scientific organisation must have increased efficiency from 25 per cent. to somewhere between 80 and 90 per cent., with the result that even at the time when raw materials were double their pre-war price and labour rates were at their highest, an automobile was produced at a price which enabled every well-paid working man in the United States to own one. This question of efficiency in the motor-car industry is not now peculiar to the United States, although it reaches its highest peak there because of the vast scale of the operations.

Henry Ford has probably done more to increase the standard of living in industrial countries than any man living. It is clear that his methods can be applied in this country. They are in fact being applied by essentially British firms and by the Ford Motor Company itself.

Now better standards of living arise either from scientific discovery or from opening up great natural resources. The case has been argued for constituting industrial science as an accurate science to be put to the service of every section of the community.

Once more the objection will be raised— How are you going to distribute all these goods without over-production? It is perfectly true that you cannot increase the purchasing power of the user of consumption goods without very complicated operations which we are attempting to describe. Total purchasing power cannot be increased by giving higher wages, because without increased efficiency higher wages mean higher costs, higher prices, and loss of trade, with consequent unemployment: purchasing power tends to decrease, and at the best remains steady. Let us get this idea clearer. So much money is paid out weekly in wages and salaries, or becomes available to the consumer of goods through dividends and profits. The bulk of this money is spent in consumption goods; the selling price of the goods must be roughly equated to the amount of money available. What happens if we increase the quantity of goods produced by 50 per cent., and if, at the same time, we reduce the average price of such goods by one-third? The total selling price of our goods is again equivalent to the total amount of wages, etc., available for buying them. It is unnecessary to examine the problem more deeply, because we are led logically to the conclusion that our aim must be to increase the efficiency of producing goods without lowering wages and with a higher price-level than that ruling to-day for raw commodities. The cost of all manufacturing operations must be reduced sufficiently by scientific reorganisation.

Naturally the process cannot be applied equally to all industries. It reaches its maximum efficiency in the production of the more highly manufactured articles such as the motor car, radio set, electrical equipment, and even in the textile industry and in iron and steel production. It cannot reach such a high degree of efficiency in the coal-mining industry, because labour enters so largely into the cost of coal-getting. Much, however, can be done even for coal, and in any case the lower prices resulting from the reorganisation of other industries would automatically give the coal-miner an increased standard of living.

To come to the point where some practical way must be found as to setting about the problem. Industries are not reorganised overnight; knowledge does not exist on how to administer and control the larger units of production. Conflicting human interests must be overcome. Success can only be obtained by general agreement regarding the course to be followed and a burning of midnight oil to obtain the requisite knowledge. The men can only be found from within the industries themselves, but their value and ability to carry on the work can be largely increased by contact with co-ordinating organisations set up by the Government in conjunction with banking and financial interests as outlined in the last chapter.

CHAPTER VIII

BUILDING A NATIONAL INDUSTRY

To build a National Industry from a hundred incohesive parts, ranging from manufacturing units to merchants' agents in distant export markets, seems a superhuman task, impossible to carry out in less than fifty years. Industries which may be described as national have generally been built up by the genius, courage, and undivided purpose of one outstanding man operating over a long period of years. Leadership, courage, and knowledge, combined in one man in such degree as to persuade all the smaller men to come in, are not very frequently available. And yet the trail has been blazed. The principles of scientific administration are becoming more definite, although they are not widely understood in the less integrated industries. A general move in the direction of national industries would quickly bring to light standardised systems of financial control, and methods of reorganising and extending sales and production, which would be rapidly absorbed by a commercial community without rival in its wide composite knowledge of the avenues of world trade. This being so, there is not the need for outstanding genius as there was before the nucleus of knowledge had been gained. Adversity is a great teacher and a great unifier. The sense of uncertainty in the present state of affairs may accomplish what fifty years of mediocre prosperity could not do.

Organisation

Let us assume that ten firms constituting a section of an industry have decided to build up one unit from their united resources, and study the possible sequence of events. The nature of their problem will vary largely according to the way in which they effect sales, because contact with the ultimate purchaser of their goods is vitally necessary in order that production may be related both in design and quantity to close estimates of the consumer's demands. If in the past the manufacturers have sold through merchants, the best of the merchants must be brought into the scheme. The day has long since gone when the manufacturer could dictate to the consumer.

From the directors of the constituent companies a central executive is formed which will be responsible for making and administering the PLAN, which will have been sketched out on the lines put forward in Chapter VI. An executive head must be chosen, whose final decision on any subject will command respect and loyalty throughout the organisation. If he cannot be found within the industry, it is better to go outside for a man who will not be subjected to petty jealousies, because, unfortunately, much of his time will be given in the initial stages to dealing with human factors from a detached viewpoint.

The executive will deal mainly with three broad lines of reorganisation: (*a*) Finance; (*b*) Commercial (Sales, Purchasing, and Commercial Research); (*c*) Technical (Production and Technical Research). Another section must be superimposed over these three, viz. Central Administration, which may vary widely, from the chairman himself, acting alone, to a committee consisting of the executive heads of the business.

The directors and staff of the constituent companies will continue to function for a time as before, and key appointments to the central organisation will be made from the local boards and staffs, as ability and special knowledge may decide. Ultimately, departments will

F

be constituted to carry out the above functions, but initially they will probably be dealt with by small working committees.

Action

The first and most important problem facing the executive will be that of finance. Considerable liquid resources will be required for additional plant in operations for standardising and concentrating production, but in many cases it should be possible to obtain sufficient cash, if it does not already exist, by making economies in stocks of raw materials and finished products held in all markets. If new capital is required, it must be obtained on the market; but as a general rule schemes involving heavy capital expenditure should not be embarked on until the organisation has settled down and production plans have been closely related to sales possibilities.

The question of total capital employed in an industry is an extremely important one. This country is fortunate at the moment in that production capacity is not at the stage of real over-production, except in the older industries, such as textiles and iron and steel. In America real over-production exists, and the capacity for manufacturing automobiles and tyres, for instance, is several times that which can be absorbed by the home market. The result is that, although individual firms may not be over-capitalised in relation to their production capacity, they are severely over-capitalised in respect of actual potential sales. This has a substantial effect on costs, since depreciation and profit figures on unproductive capital tend to increase selling prices. Owing to low share prices, the present moment appears to be ideal in British industry for writing down the capitalisation of a combination of companies to a figure which can be justified by the value of their actual productive assets.

On the commercial side two immediate lines of investigation and action will be followed. In the first place, the raw material requirements (including fuel and packing materials) will be thoroughly overhauled and a central purchasing department organised which will place all major contracts. In the second place, a review will be made of all possible markets with the idea of cutting down consignment stocks and of eliminating redundant agencies. The ultimate ideal for the selling organisation is to have direct representation in every market which can justify the cost of the organisation required, and thus bring the ultimate consumer and knowledge of his requirements into cable contact with the production end.

The technical organisation can consider immediately the concentration of production to a certain extent. In the case we are considering it is assumed that there are ten factories each of which is running at about half-capacity. It should be possible to close four of these with considerable economy and reduction of unit cost. The measures taken at this stage, however, would not necessarily be permanent. Ultimately more capacity would be required, and the question of whether this would be obtained by further concentration and by spending new capital, or by opening up factories temporarily closed down, would be a matter for the mature judgment of the central administration. It is obviously advisable to constitute a research department immediately. It would not deal at the commencement of its career with problems which could only be solved in the distant future. The problems to which it could direct its attention should be the elimination of waste by improvement of machinery, manufacturing process, and raw materials. It should also extend its study to new possible markets for the products which require technical work before those markets can be attained, and to the utilisation of by-products in order to reduce cost of raw material.

Within a year of the establishment of the central body, the commercial and technical departments, working in daily touch, should have in readiness a plan for standardisation of the company's products. This would be made as a result of the market investigations initiated by the commercial department with the object of cutting down the number of varieties of the company's product to a minimum, and making that minimum in such a way as to meet the consumer's needs.

The final stage of reorganisation would then be embarked on, involving maximum economies in every direction, with standardisation as complete as possible, and reduction of price to increase the demand.

Results

In the table on page 86 the nature and extent of economies have been considered in detail. The product to which the table refers is taken from an engineering trade which is not at present rationalised, and which would be susceptible to the sequence of events described

A Consideration of the Nature of Cost Reductions which might be Effected by Scientific Reorganisation of the Commercial Operations of Ten Similar Plants

I. In one year with $12\frac{1}{2}$ per cent. increase of production.

II. In five years with 50 per cent. increase of production.

Cost Item	Before Reorganisation	I	II
Raw materials	32	27	21
Services (power, gas, water)..	3	$2\frac{1}{2}$	2
Repairs and maintenance ..	2	$1\frac{1}{2}$	$1\frac{1}{2}$
Direct wages	24	18	14
Rates and insurance	2	$1\frac{1}{2}$	$1\frac{1}{2}$
Works overhead charges ..	10	7	4
Carriage and freight	2	2	$1\frac{1}{2}$
Advertising	4	4	$2\frac{1}{2}$
Selling expenses	10	9	5
Administration	5	8	$5\frac{1}{2}$
Obsolescence	4	$4\frac{1}{2}$	3
Profit (subject to tax) ..	2	5	10
Wholesale selling price ..	100	90	72

The ratio of capital to turnover is taken to be unity throughout, additional plant being financed from obsolescence and other reserves.

above. The first column indicates the way in which the selling price of the article is made up-to-date. The second column indicates the results which might be attained at the end of the first year of combined operation with nine firms of similar size; and the third column indicates the results which might be obtained at the end of five years or less when scientific methods of control have been introduced throughout.

I. The following assumptions are made with regard to results at the end of the first year:

(*a*) That production is increased by $12\frac{1}{2}$ per cent. and price reduced by 10 per cent.

(*b*) That the cost of raw materials has been reduced by approximately 15 per cent. by the company being able to place larger and more uniform contracts, by elimination of waste, disposal of scrap, and to a greater measure of standardisation.

(*c*) The wages have been reduced by 25 per cent. per unit of production through closing down 40 per cent. of the factories and greater efficiency in the remainder.

(*d*) Reduction in works overhead charges is taken at somewhat the same ratio.

(*e*) That the cost of advertising and propaganda will have increased slightly in total, although ultimately it should be possible to get an immensely greater effect from the same expenditure of money devoted to clear-cut lines instead of being dispersed over ten different firms.

(*f*) Selling charges remain at about the same total, although slightly reduced per unit of production.

(*g*) Administration has been nearly doubled in order to allow for expansion of staff required by the central executive.

(*h*) The figure for obsolescence per unit has been increased by a half per cent., and the assumption is made that during the first year 20 per cent. is added to the figure on the books for plant, in respect of new plant and reorganisation of existing material.

(*i*) It is assumed that the average profit of the companies entering the combine is only 2 per cent., and that this should rise to 5 per cent. at the end of the first year. It may be asked why prices should be reduced so much and the profit limited to 5 per cent. The explanation is that we have budgeted for an increase of production of 12½ per cent., and that, with trade conditions remaining the same, a price reduction of 10 per cent. would be necessary to enable this increase to be disposed of.

II. The following assumptions are made with regard to the results at the end of five years, when the maximum economies have been made consistent with an increase in output of 50 per cent.

(*a*) It is assumed that production has been increased by 50 per cent. and that the average selling price of the goods has been lowered by $33\frac{1}{3}$ per cent. The actual economies shown would only allow for a price reduction of 28 per cent., assuming that a 10 per cent. profit were now being made. It is considered, however, that the difference should be made up by the retailer sacrificing a portion of his normal profit per unit, which he should be able to do with the increased mass of business which he would be handling.

(*b*) *Raw Materials.*—It is now assumed that price reductions have been made in all raw materials used by the industry into which manufacturing operations have entered. Further economies will have been made in utilisation of materials and alternative products chosen which give the same result at lower cost. The best market will have been found for scrap.

(c) The further reduction of wages cost per unit is quite consistent with fully standardised production. It should be pointed out, however, that the total number of men employed has probably not varied much over the period. The number of men to whom direct wages are paid has been reduced by about 13 per cent., but this proportion would be fully taken up in additional labour required for repairs and maintenance, and in the employment outside the industry of more men in respect of raw materials and transport. It should also be indicated that the process of rationalisation involves the employment of a greater proportion of clerks and of more highly paid individuals, so that continual recruitment from working-class families to positions requiring a higher standard of education would result.

(d) *Selling.*—It is now assumed that selling charges per unit have been cut in half, and that the total cost of disposing of the company's production has been reduced by 25 per cent. of the expenditure of the ten original companies in that respect. This will be recognised by those who have made similar economies as a reasonable figure which could easily be exceeded.

(e) The cost of administration remains in

total at about the same figure as that taken in the first year. The problems of the central administration should not become more difficult or complicated after a period of five years, and the cost should be reduced if anything.

The net results of the operations described above are that the production of 50 per cent. more goods has been accomplished and that cost of production and distribution has been reduced to such an extent that the necessary price reductions can be made to ensure the sale of the goods. An unprofitable industry paying no dividends has also been turned into an industry giving reasonable profit, whose preference and ordinary shares should stand at or above par.

If we could have to-day the results of mature consideration from each section of industry as to whether anything like these results could be obtained in practice, we should have the reply to our question, "Can the unemployment problem be solved and the general standard of living increased by at least 50 per cent.?"

COMMERCIAL RESEARCH

Research is the foundation of scientific achievement. It is the basis of every branch of science, and without it material progress would be impossible. To collect thousands of apparently unrelated details, to weave them into theories, to try out the theories experimentally on a small scale, to discard what is not true or useful, and, finally, to establish a smoothly working sequence of correlated actions—that is research.

Commercial science is in some ways more difficult than chemical, physical, or mathematical science; in other ways, fortunately, it is more simple. In chemical or physical research not only is a definite, rigid law discovered, but exact limits are deduced for every stage of the new reactions brought into service. Abstruse mathematical calculations and wide scientific knowledge are required from the research worker. In commercial research, on the other hand, a similar degree of accurate deduction is impossible. The human element enters into all observations, and to forecast 90 per cent.

of the truth can be regarded as a good result for a single investigation. However, the mathematical problems involved rarely require more than the four simple rules of arithmetic, and good commercial knowledge combined with common sense forms the best mental equipment. Fortunately, these attributes are not lacking in any of our industries.

The most urgent need for research at the present time is the relation of gold to the problem of the maximum possible production and exchange of goods. Gold is the promoter and controller of all trade—the catalyst. But, as the chemist researches until he finds the best way in which to use a catalyst, so the financial expert and economist must find a sure method to control the use of gold in order that the good it can do in building an enduring prosperity for the world may be obtained.

Gold is a noble metal. Scientists will agree that it is a fit subject for the scientific method. We must, however, descend the scale of commercial research, and outline the types of knowledge required by a manufacturing company before it can reach its maximum of prosperity.

Research and the National Industry

I. The first series of investigation deals with two aspects of the sales problem:

(i) The total market attainable.
(ii) A sales forecast for a year.

Both estimates are built up by special investigators or by means of carefully constructed questionnaires to the company's selling agents. The result of the investigations will be an answer to such questions as the following:

(*a*) What is the estimated market for each item of the company's production in every country where it seems possible to compete?

(*b*) At what rate can this market be obtained, assuming that a progressive policy is followed?

(*c*) What is the best sales organisation for each market, and what will it cost?

(*d*) Who are the principal competitors in each market? What advantages or disadvantages have they?

(*e*) What are the right methods to be followed in attaining the objective—e.g. finish of goods, methods of packing, advertising, delivery, etc.?

(*f*) What stocks must be held in each market?

(*g*) What credit must be given?

Research and Budgetary Control

II. With the answers to the above questions in their hands, the executive can plan production. It is assumed that an effective statistical system has been evolved which will enable the sales forecast to be translated into a policy for every department of the organisation. A budget is prepared for a year's operations. The responsibility for each section of expense in the company's activities must be clearly fixed, and each individual who bears such responsibility must make every effort to keep within the allocated figure, and to examine at all times any possibility of reducing it. To realise the net profit estimated in the budget will thus depend on the sense of responsibility of everyone from the chairman to the foremen. The budget must be flexible. Its results must be examined at monthly intervals, and every item be readjusted if the sales forecast is either not being realised or is being surpassed. Otherwise stocks of raw material and manufactured products will become either excessive or inadequate, and cost will not bear the right relation to sales price.

It is outside our scope to discuss at length the action to be taken by the whole organisation when the sales forecast has been made up, but the following questions require further research.

(*a*) How is production to be reorganised to give steady output of goods which are standardised as far as the requirements of various markets will permit?

(*b*) How can raw-material contracts be arranged to the best advantage in order to give flexibility of delivery and progressive reduction of cost with increasing output?

(*c*) What technical research must be carried out to evolve new types of goods which the sales investigation has shown will be required?

III. With the end of the first year's operations much experience will have been gained. Inaccuracies will have come to light. Inexperienced operators of the system of control by budget will have discovered how to increase the accuracy of their forecasts. They will gain enthusiasm and team spirit. A system will be in operation by which men can gain rapid promotion because their results can be measured. The executive at all times has full knowledge of the potentialities of every market open to the products of the company. It can, moreover, estimate the results which may be attainable in terms of net profits, which are in the end the sole criterion of success.

Research in Merchandising

In the somewhat detailed and technical suggestions of the preceding chapters, little reference has been made to the question of Retail Distribution. The selling price of the manufacturer or producer is the cost price of the retailer, who has to add his own expenses and profit in order to fix the price which the consumer pays. In some cases the expenses and profits of one or more intermediaries are interposed between manufacturer and retailer, and the total cost of distribution is thus inflated to an unreasonable extent. Commercial research, carried out by co-operation between a national unit of industry and the larger retailers can undoubtedly create efficient distribution and afford the means to attain the considerable price reductions which are necessary to provide the higher standard of living which we desire. The directions in which research can be best applied are as follows:

(*a*) To reduce the number of lines stocked by the retailer.

This problem presents an easy solution when the retailer has to buy a particular commodity from one firm instead of from ten manufacturers competing for his custom. Retailer and manufacturer can arrange between them a minimum number of lines which will meet the requirements of the consumer. They can, moreover, arrange to increase the quality, finish, and general desirability of such lines and to reduce their cost.

(*b*) To minimise the amount of stock held by the retailer.

The price of an article is increased if it has to be held in stock for a long time because of intermittent demand. Here also the reduction of the number of lines stocked and an increase in their desirability because of improved style and finish enable the retailer to hold a much lower proportion of stock in relation to sales. The retailer is also in direct touch with the manufacturer, who has always adequate stocks on hand and can guarantee supplies at a few hours' notice. This would be quite impossible if the retailer were buying from several competitive sources based on unstandardised production.

(*c*) To reduce the cost of the distributing system.

We have seen that substantial savings are made in the manufacturer's cost of selling to the retailer when many firms combine together. The ultimate effect of reducing the number of manufacturing units and of the simultaneous growth of large chain stores will be that unnecessary intermediaries will be eliminated and that the commercial traveller will become as extinct as the dodo. He will be replaced by experts belonging to the manufacturing or distributing organisation, who will form a link between the wishes of the public and the means of production. The ultimate effect will be to reduce distributing costs to a minimum.

Men

Commercial research, therefore, is the foundation of the scientific reorganisation of industry. It may fairly be asked, "Where can we obtain the trained men to build up and operate such a complicated mechanism?" The answer is—that there exist within any group of companies sufficient men of innate ability and sound business knowledge to grasp the main principles of the science they themselves are going to build up, and that science, once understood, simplifies and does not complicate. Expert advice must be found from a central source such as the advisory organisation envisaged in Chapter VI. Such schools as the London School of Economics (Department of Business Administration) will provide young recruits highly trained theoretically, and only requiring a few years' experience to make them of outstanding value in the industries which they join.

To help to build a national industry; to have a clear objective at which to aim; to know the methods by which the objective may be attained—these are the rewards which commercial research may give to a man.

REVIEW OF BRITISH INDUSTRIES

The state of scientific efficiency in our industries varies so widely that in trying to present a uniform method of reorganisation we lay ourselves open to the criticism of being theoretical and unpractical. The extent to which the method is used and the form of organisation which it creates present, however, an almost infinite variety. The main objective is always the same—to discover the widest market attainable by an industry and to make an efficient production plan from which wasteful effort and redundant expenditure are eliminated. Let us examine quite briefly the direction which reorganisation might take in some of the larger industries.

(a) Coal

Coal comes first to our thoughts. None of our problems present greater difficulties. Labour bulks so largely in the cost of production, and wages must not be cut. The industry provides a huge export, and so helps to maintain the balance of trade; it provides freight and fuel for our ships; it is the basis of a network of electric power which promises to be incomparable; it feeds the coke ovens and blast furnaces of a great steel industry which is on the threshold of revival. It is obvious that coal is our life-blood. There is no room for loose thinking or compromise in this matter. Cost of production must be brought to the lowest possible point, in order that the industries depending on coal may prosper. It can only be done by a national policy: by grouping the pits—by eliminating those where costs are high and by using modern machinery where costs are low; by combining in export sales organisation and avoiding overlap in domestic distribution. There is no excuse for a system which brings coal carts from six competing distributors down the same street. Finally, there are methods of utilising coal within the country which can redress our trade balance with America as surely as the export of coal itself would do. By the direct hydrogenation of coal under high pressure it can be converted into fuel oil or petrol of the highest grade. Such an achievement by British technicians should be followed up by production on a sufficiently large scale to affect employment and to promote further discovery. By low temperature carbonisation a smokeless household fuel is obtained, together with a small proportion of oil and gas. This method also has its applications, provided that the gas can be sold at a fair figure to gas undertakings. The final aim of the scientist is to make powdered coal take the place of oil in the internal-combustion engine. If this came about coal would become a greater national asset than it has ever been.

(b) Iron and Steel

The iron and steel industry, and with it shipbuilding, were born of our rich deposits of coal and iron-stone. The latter raw material is not entirely adequate, and iron ore has to be imported to some extent. These industries, however, are a magnificent framework on which to build an enormous trade in the home and export markets, with hardly any tribute to foreign countries. What is the physical condition of that framework? Germany, Belgium, France, have built large-scale units of production since the War by means of depreciated currencies. America erected still larger plants during her long spell of post-war prosperity. The former countries had by 1927 increased their export trade in iron and steel by 70 per cent. over their pre-war figure. British exports had hardly expanded at all. The cause of this disparity was mainly connected with the financial rectitude of Great Britain, whose policy of meeting all liabilities and remaining on the Gold Standard made capital and labour charges, and taxation, consistently higher than the Continental steel manufacturer had to face, and prevented plant development. The British steel industry is not, however, down and out. It has, during the past few years been undergoing a process of amalgamation and concentration of manufactures which must have reduced costs considerably. It possesses leaders of great ability who will see the necessary reorganisation through. The imports of iron and steel into this country have risen to above 3,000,000 tons per annum, the production of which would give employment to 60,000 men. It does not seem too much to hope that in due course these imports will be produced in England, but it is not a problem which can be solved merely by the imposition of a tariff. New plants must be built, perfectly sited and planned to obtain both the increased domestic market *without increase of selling price to the manufacturer of finished goods*, and also a more substantial share of the export market. England still remains an ideal country for producing iron and steel economically, and her metallurgists and engineers are still in the van of technical progress. There is sufficient initiative and ability within the industry to produce a rational plan of production between the manufacturing groups and an export sales organisation which will leave no stone unturned in the search for new avenues of trade. The steel industry will come back.

(c) Textiles

The British textile industries, producing cotton, woollen, linen, and artificial silk goods, merit an expert analysis beyond the scope of this work or the knowledge of the writer. Their products have still the best reputation for quality in the world markets. They still make large contributions to the export trade, but the great cotton markets of the East have been partially captured by domestic manufacture and by Japan, and the British market itself has been subjected to the gradual infiltration of substantial quantities of Continental textiles. The reasons are manifold. To begin with, unit wages, capital costs, and taxation have been too high. These factors are in process of adjustment with the fall in sterling, and some of the advantage may be permanently retained. The only certainty of permanently regaining competitive power, however, is by complete and scientific reorganisation.

The textile groups share certain features of organisation. Their raw material goes to the spinner who produces yarn, the spinner sells yarn to the manufacturer, who weaves the cloth; the cloth goes to the bleacher and finisher, who gives it its final form before it is sent to the market. At some stage of the manufacturing process the goods become the property of the merchant who may distribute in the home market or sell to another merchant abroad. In view of the vast number of firms engaged it is obvious that planned production, using the principles outlined in the last chapter, cannot take place. If it did, it would not be surprising to see an average reduction in the cost of the finished article amounting to between 20 and 30 per cent. Briefly expressed, the nature of the reorganisation which the textile industries require to undergo is as follows:

(i) Formation of subsections of industry based on similar classes of goods, each section containing merchants, manufacturers, and spinners with a close working agreement with the finishers (who are already organised), i.e. a vertical combination for each class of goods.

(ii) An organisation for each section capable of forming a sales forecast for every market and working out a definite production plan.

(iii) An overriding organisation to deal with matters of broad policy such as tariff questions and co-operative manufacture in foreign markets (e.g. China and India) in conjunction with the importation of higher-class goods.

(iv) A clear understanding with labour that for critical export markets wages costs should be reduced to a minimum by operating as many looms as possible to the weaver.

The reorganisation of the textile industries is the most difficult problem we have to face, but if a clear-cut objective is agreed upon, it will be a very important step forward.

(d) Agriculture

The reorganisation of farming in the United Kingdom demands as much clear thinking as the textile industry. The country produces little more than one-third of its food require-ments. It is within the bounds of a practicable plan to double this amount. The arable farmer has, under the Free Trade system, always been at the mercy of world conditions, and with grain prices at their 1931 level his plight is a desperate one. The dairy farmer has been able to survive because his main product—milk—is not directly subjected to foreign com-petition. The pig farmer has suffered from violent price fluctuation from year to year. These have prevented the growth of a stable industry which could place standardised pro-ducts on the markets to compete with the £50,000,000 of pig products imported annually. Farming as a whole could be put on a stable basis by a scheme involving controlled imports and regulated prices. It is no use avoiding the issue of higher prices, but the increase need not be unduly heavy if scientific methods of operation and organisation are brought into play. The production and marketing of food requires a higher degree of efficient organisa-tion than any manufacturing industry.

(i) The farmer, in the first place, has the means of efficient production available. With the certainty of realising a profit if prices are fixed, he will adopt more intensive methods, and by employing the maximum useful quantity of fertilisers, and the advantages of mechanisation, costs will be reduced considerably. Great discoveries have been made which are enabling this intensification to be carried out.

(ii) The products of the farmer should be sold to the marketing organisation with a fair and steady profit to the farmer of average efficiency. The marketing organisation must then build up a degree of efficiency which will allow it to work on a continually reducing margin of cost, with a fair profit on the capital actually employed. The present system allows an increasing disparity between wholesale and retail prices to be built up which penalises the farmer on the one hand and the consumer on the other. Many economies would be realised by an organisation working on a national scale. It would know the total available market. It could prevent the farmer from over-producing. It could keep its factory operations running at a regular pace and work up all by-products to their maximum value. It would prevent unnecessary movement of commodities. All these are patent cost factors, and efficiency in any direction will tend to reduce retail prices.

The problems of reorganisation involved may be insuperable, but the issue is clear. Distributing companies, with well-defined responsibility, high technical efficiency, and a national outlook, operating on the basis of a guaranteed price to the farmer, will go far to restore prosperity and purchasing power to the country-side. The imports of feeding-stuffs, meat, cheese, butter, and fruit would still be sufficient to satisfy the Dominions, and shipping would not be affected to an extent which might appear probable at first sight.

A note on agriculture would be incomplete at the present time without reference to the rapidly evolving canning industry, which can be an example of what an efficient manufacturing and distributing unit can do for the farming community.

(e) Building

Between two and three hundred million pounds are spent annually on building operations in the United Kingdom. More than one-half of this sum is for direct labour, and of the component products the bulk are made in the country from domestic raw materials. It is therefore of prime importance that the quality and quantity of buildings should be increased, and the cost reduced, in order that the replanning of out-of-date and unsanitary housing may be carried out without cost to the State.

(i) The production of building materials must be planned on the lines indicated in previous chapters. There is great scope here, and an example of what is possible is given by the replacing of unstandardised wooden window-frames by the admirable metal frames which have been evolved. The cost of such items as roofing tiles, baths and other sanitary ware, paint and varnish, doors and flooring materials, is considerably reduced when the product is standardised and subjected to mass production and distribution by national units of industry. It is just as possible for the best and most artistic product to be made by these methods as the cheap and inartistic type. An average reduction of 20 per cent. in the cost of certain types of building materials should be obtainable.

(ii) In building operations labour can make an enormous contribution to scientific efficiency. If the results of motion study were applied throughout, the cost of finished buildings could be considerably reduced, even although individual earnings were increased.

(iii) Some co-ordinating organisation is required, to regulate production as between each section of the industry and at the same time to produce or encourage continuous improvement, in design of buildings, and in town planning. Its formation would be a matter for agreement between Government and industry.

(f) Electrical Industries

Thanks to the comparatively modern development of the industries producing electrical equipment, they are already well organised into units of considerable size, linked together by trade associations which tend to promote the "National" outlook. Nearly every section holds its own in the export markets, and it may be taken for granted that the industry as a whole will remain in the forefront of the advance towards scientific reorganisation. The grid system, organised nationally under the Central Electricity Board, forms a model of economical distribution. The result is that electric current is becoming universally available at a price which makes the use of electrical equipment an increasingly attractive proposition in the factory and the home. Not only does the grid system provide for present needs. It has already placed the heavy end of the industry, i.e. that section which manufactures plant, in a position to gain an increasing share of world markets. The next stage will be a great access of activity in the manufacture of standardised equipment for using electricity in the home. The equipment thus produced may be expected to fall rapidly in price as it is produced in greater quantity, with the result that the industry will become a progressively greater employer of labour. The manufacturers of wireless equipment have demonstrated recently how rapid progress may be with regard both to quality and price reduction, but they would do well to adopt a co-operative national organisation to deal with the export trade, by the manufacture of standardised products suitable for every attainable market.

(g) Motor Transport

The invention and development of new features in mechanical transport are particularly well suited to the British character. In spite of the enormous size of the American companies and the financial resources of the research organisations they employ, technical progress in Great Britain will bear comparison with that in the United States. We are still under-organised for production, however, with the result that foreign and even Dominion markets have not yet been obtained in competition with America. In order to consolidate our position larger units of production are necessary and a definite overseas programme. These can only be obtained by further amalgamations within the industry. There is a great reward to be gained. Motor transport outside the United States is everywhere underdeveloped, and the British industry can still, if it will, obtain a commanding position in export markets.

(h) General

The field of possibility has hardly been touched in this brief review of the problems of reorganisation which lie before our industries. In general, however, these problems seem to sort themselves into two classes—to reorganise the older industries into far fewer units of production and sales, and to stimulate the newer industries so that they seize their opportunities, quickly and on as great a scale as possible. The driving force in both these movements can only come from knowledge of what may be attained, and research to find the methods of attainment. There is no complete political remedy: nothing can be done by compulsion: only hard work and the national resources of ability and character can regain the prestige occupied by British industry in the nineteenth century and hold it fast.

CHAPTER XI

THE RATIONALISED STATE

The advent of mass production and of organised methods of distribution meant the end of individualism for the majority. Individualism in the future will be mainly for the artist and the philosopher, and so far as the economic life of the country is concerned, we must make the best of a system based on collective effort in most spheres of activity. Unless the chief industrial countries can remedy the mistakes into which the confused policies of the present century have driven them, the outlook is extremely gloomy. The consequences of those mistakes are upon them, however, and as they are neither threatened by a barbarian invasion from without nor by a collapse of moral fibre within, they are likely to find a rational solution somewhat on the lines we have endeavoured to describe. The Rationalised Capitalist State is probably the only alternative to Bolshevism.

Russia

In considering this question the mind naturally turns to Russia. What of the Communist Five-Year Plan? Are we not advocating a system which will lead to a world which will be an easy prey to Communism? The downfall of Communism in Italy, Germany, and other European States during the few years following the War gives a negative answer to this vital question. Communism cannot expect to succeed even in Russia, and although the Five-Year Plan commenced on a Communist basis, it is likely to end with some measure of success, under a modified system of payment by results and according to ability, which will slowly but definitely lead Russia back to the private ownership of wealth—the basis of the capitalist system. It will not be the same social system as that ruling in other countries. The Bolshevist experiment has been too profound to allow that. The capitalist countries are unlikely to copy an economic system which breaks down at every turn because it does not utilise the fundamental acquisitive instincts of its members so as to build up its national wealth. Russia was virgin ground for a great economic experiment after the Revolution. Her industries were non-existent; her citizens had no property; her peasants had been virtually slaves. In 1923 Chicherin, at the Foreign Office in Moscow, outlined to a trade mission, including the writer, the social objective of the Soviets. He illustrated his theme by means of three diagrams in which the vertical portion represented individual incomes and the horizontal portion the number of people enjoying such incomes.

(1) Czarist Russia was represented as follows:

The people, with the exception of a fraction of 1 per cent., enjoyed merely the privilege of living, with hardly the means to do so. The few possessed wealth in abundance.

(2) The United States of America were represented by a triangle:

The graduations of income range in easy
stages from the largest and poorest class who

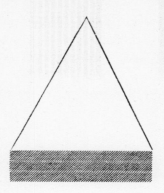

are, however, well above the subsistence line
to a still numerous class of the very wealthy
represented by the top portion of the triangle.

(3) The Soviet Ideal:

The third diagram was a simple one. It
represented a uniform income for the whole
population, raised to the highest figure, which
the efficiency of production would allow. The
£200-a-year State.

The ideal has already broken down. Efficiency in the worker has to be rewarded. Income beyond that required for living can be saved. Savings, even though they must be invested in compulsory State loans, become capital and gradually lead to the idea of private ownership. Considerable inequality of income will ultimately be built up, and although State control of the means of production may persist in Russia, a bourgeois and a leisured class is ultimately likely to emerge.

The Rationalised Capitalist State

Without any radical political experiment, without changing the nature of society, and without taking from any man the opportunity to make wealth both for himself and the community, it is possible to build up in the British Empire and in other countries a scientific organisation for the production, distribution, and exchange of goods. Whether it will actually be brought about will depend mainly on two factors. Firstly, political and industrial leaders must agree that it constitutes a practicable and desirable policy. Secondly, the rank and file must be convinced, and must subordinate their immediate interests to the requirements of a common plan.

Under a scientifically organised State there would be no greater loss of freedom or individuality than is the case to-day with those serving in great industrial corporations. Art and Science would be encouraged and utilised in order that buildings, decoration, design, and inventions should make continual progress. After a period of strenuous effort during the process of reconstruction it should be possible to return to more pleasant and less competitive conditions in which, however, the interest of working with definite objectives under a simplified system should be sufficient to prevent the community from social decay.

CHAPTER XII

RECAPITULATION

The nations of the world to-day may be compared to a family of people on the verge of a nervous breakdown. For restoration of industrial vitality nothing more is required than recognition of the causes of the trouble and will-power to recover. The diagnosis is now a matter of general agreement, and if the calm sanity which is expected from national leaders asserts itself, and if Press and public opinion in every country give their support, international action should be taken within a few months which will aim to restore the basis of confidence. The interests of every living man are the same in this matter.

It is, therefore, probable that Reparations and War Debts will be scaled down.

The question of remonetisation of silver should be settled in the best interests of general prosperity.

Effective measures should be taken to raise the price-level of primary commodities.

Speculation should be restricted by international agreement.

Finally, an international credit system must be built up which will prevent any possibility of a further breakdown of the Gold Standard and form the basis of a steady price-level and permanent advance in prosperity throughout the world.

All these things can be accomplished within reasonable time. And what then?

Science has advanced very far; yet not far enough! She has already made possible a new world of material things for every man to enjoy if he can find the way. She has explored the universe and measured accurately the movements and physical condition of myriads of stars. But she has neither made nor attempted to make a system which will work for regulating the results of man's enterprise and skill.

The purpose of these few pages has been to set out a problem which will remain unsolved when the present world crisis has been successfully overcome. It is the problem of the maximum profitable production of goods in the common interest, and it calls for a degree of scientific achievement which will rival that of the long line of illustrious discoverers which this country has produced.

From the international point of view the chief difficulties to be overcome are outlined above. But from the national, or rather imperial, standpoint the solution of the problem involves industrial research and planning which transcends by far the importance of regaining comparative prosperity by the uncontrolled flow of natural forces. I have attempted in brief space to set out a method which aims at building up national units of industry characterised by management, perfectly informed regarding the means of economic production and the maximum attainable market. The reward of success in such an endeavour would be to regain preeminence in most branches of industry and commerce, and to create a system from which every class of the community could draw far greater rewards than are possible to-day.

Britain is at the parting of the ways. Before the crisis, when trade was as normal as it could be within ten years of the War, unemployment was increasing steadily. After the crisis, unemployment will still continue. A tariff system and a policy of economic nationalism to bring the Empire into line with the rest of the world may benefit most of our industries. But the greatest achievement of all can only be obtained by a common impulse throughout the nation to co-operate in a great movement to simplify and reanimate our commercial system, and to lead on towards a world-wide relaxation of restrictions on the freer exchange of goods.

Here is work for the generations to come; to discover, to plan, to lead, as the history of our race teaches us they will be able to do.

INDEX